COMEDY SONGS FOR WOMEN

To access recorded accompaniments online visit:
www.halleonard.com/mylibrary

Enter Code
2365-6964-8147-5074

ISBN 978-1-4950-8815-5

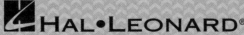

HAL•LEONARD®

7777 W. BLUEMOUND RD. P.O. BOX 13819 MILWAUKEE, WI 53213

Visit Hal Leonard Online at
www.halleonard.com

HOW TO USE HAL LEONARD ONLINE AUDIO

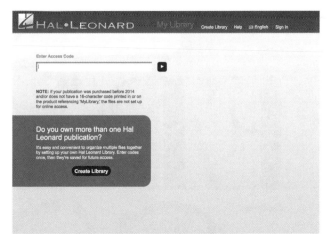

Because of the changing use of media, and the fact that fewer people are using CDs, we have made a shift to companion audio accessible online. In many cases, rather than a book with CD, we now have a book with an access code for online audio, including performances, accompaniments or diction lessons. Each copy of each book has a unique access code. We call this Hal Leonard created system "My Library." It's simple to use.

Go to www.halleonard.com/mylibrary and enter the unique access code found on page one of a relevant book/audio package.

The audio tracks can be streamed or downloaded. If you download the tracks on your computer, you can add the files to a CD or to your digital music library, and use them anywhere without being online. See below for comments about Apple and Android mobile devices.

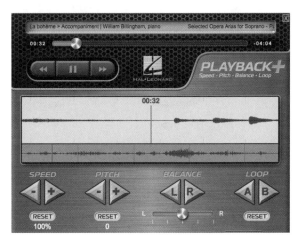

There are some great benefits to the My Library system. *Playback+* is exclusive to Hal Leonard, and when connected to the Internet with this multi-functional audio player you can:

• Change tempo without changing pitch
• Transpose to any key

Optionally, you can create a My Library account, and store all the companion audio you have purchased there. Access your account online at any time, from any device, by logging into your account at www.halleonard.com/mylibrary. Technical help may be found at www.halleonard.com/mylibrary/help/

Apple/iOS

Question: On my iPad and iPhone, the Download links just open another browser tab and play the track. How come this doesn't really download?

Answer: The Safari iOS browser will not allow you to download audio files directly in iTunes or other apps. There are several ways to work around this:

• You can download normally on your desktop computer, saving the files to iTunes. Then, you can sync your iOS device directly to your computer, or sync your iTunes content using an iCloud account.
• There are many third-party apps which allow you to download files from websites into the app's own file manager for easy retrieval and playback.

Android

Files are always downloaded to the same location, which is a folder usually called "Downloads" (this may vary slightly depending on what browser is used (Chrome, Firefox, etc)). Chrome uses a system app called "Downloads" where files can be accessed at any time. Firefox and some other browsers store downloaded files within a "Downloads" folder in the browser itself.

Recently-downloaded files can be accessed from the Notification bar; swiping down will show the downloaded files as a new "card", which you tap on to open. Opening a file depends on what apps are installed on the Android device. Audio files are opened in the device's default audio app. If a file type does not have a default app assigned to it, the Android system alerts the user.

Pianists on the recordings: [1] Brian Dean [2] Brendan Fox [3] Christopher Ruck [4] Ruben Piirainen [5] Richard Walters

The price of this publication includes access to companion recorded
accompaniments online, for download or streaming, using the unique code printed on the title page.
Visit www.halleonard.com/mylibrary and enter the access code.

ALTO'S LAMENT

Lyrics by Marcy Heisler
Music by Zina Goldrich

"The Sound of Music"

sick of, "Can't help lov-in' that man__ of mine." Just look at "O - kla - ho - ma" for ex - am - ple. That rous-ing ti - tled num-ber of the show. While ev - 'ry - one is sing-ing, "O - kla - ho - ma" I get, "Sky - y - y - y - y - y - y - y. Yo - ho!"

(Spoken:) And now a medley of my finer roles.

The

ALWAYS A BRIDESMAID

from *I Love You, You're Perfect, Now Change*

Lyrics by Joe DiPietro
Music by Jimmy Roberts

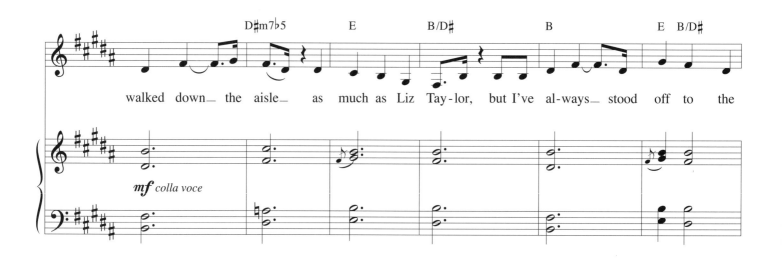

GETTING MARRIED TODAY

from *Company*

Music and Lyrics by
Stephen Sondheim

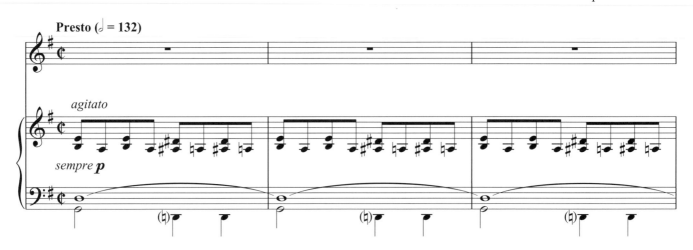

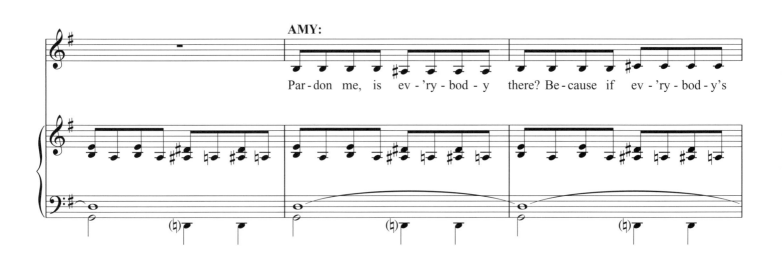

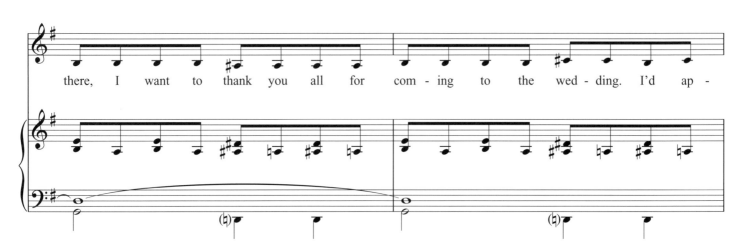

This ensemble has been adapted as a solo for this edition with the composer's blessing.

day. Go! Can't you
go? Why is no - Bod - y lis - ten - ing? Good -
bye! Go and cry At an - oth - er per - son's
wake. If you're quick, For a kick, You could

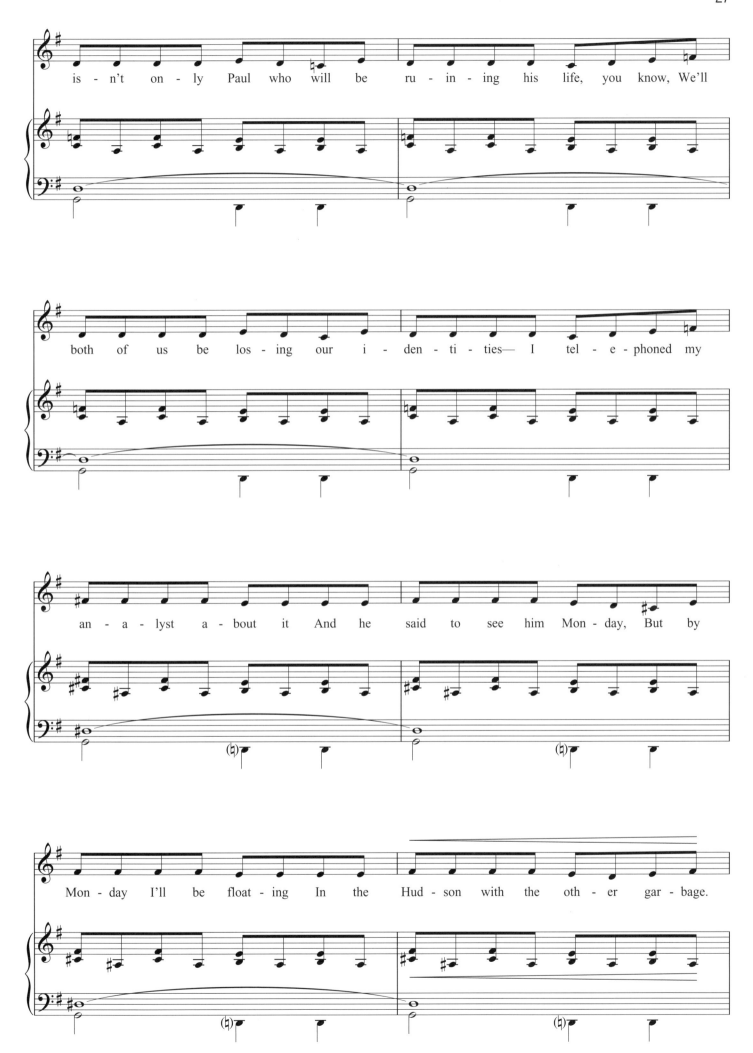

I AM PLAYING ME

from [title of show]

Words and Music by
Jeff Bowen

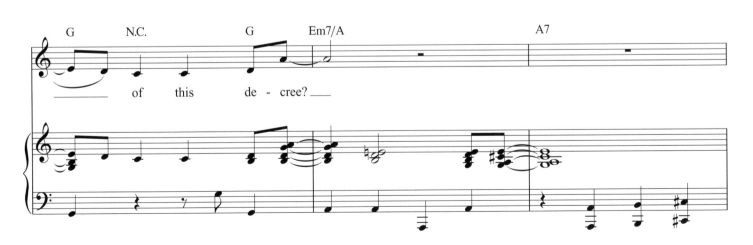

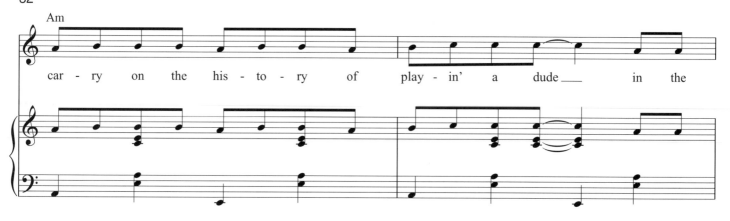

car - ry on the his - to - ry of play - in' a dude ___ in the

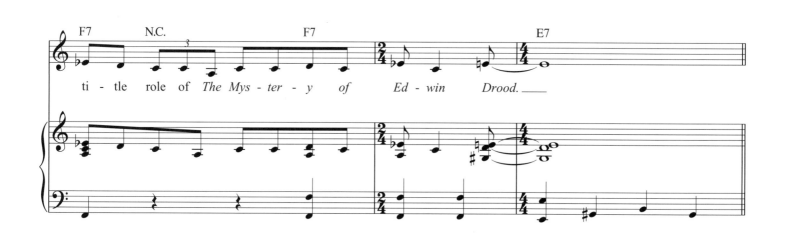

ti - tle role of *The Mys - ter - y of Ed - win Drood.* ___

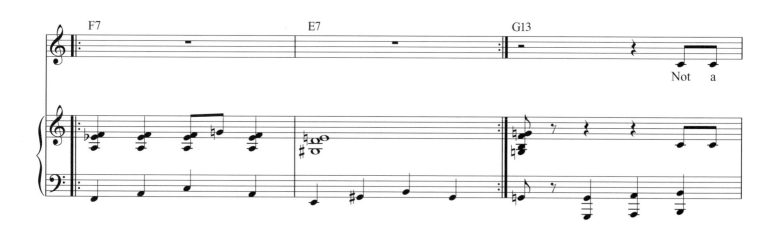

Not a

chance for my ca - reer to ad - vance ___ and there's no straight guys here for

MY NEW PHILOSOPHY
from *You're a Good Man, Charlie Brown*

Music and Lyrics by
Andrew Lippa

SALLY: *Spoken (before the vamp): "Why are you telling me?"* (beat) *I like it.*

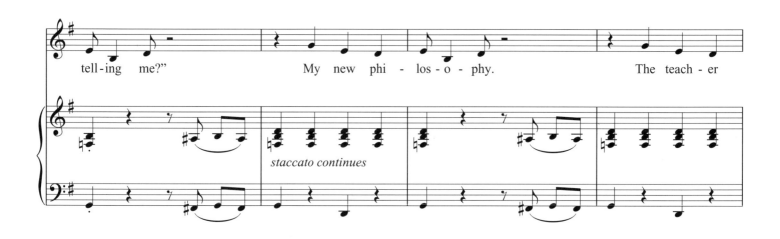

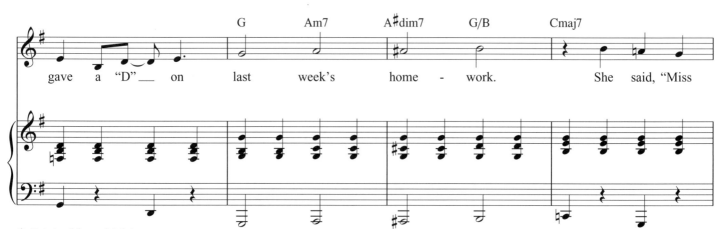

* *Original key: A Major.*
The song is a duet for Sally and Schroeder. The composer created this solo edition for publication.

NOTHING

from *A Chorus Line*

Music by Marvin Hamlisch
Lyric by Edward Kleban

Easy 2 - Rock feel
DIANA:

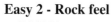

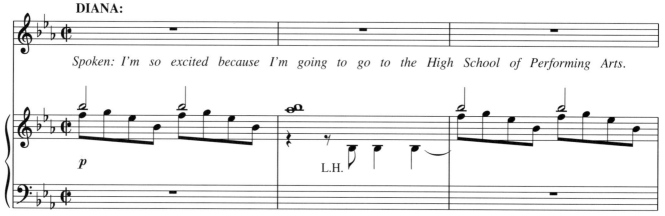

Spoken: I'm so excited because I'm going to go to the High School of Performing Arts.

I mean, I was dying to be a serious actress. Anyway it's the first day of acting class and we're in the

auditorium and the teacher, Mister Karp, puts us up on the stage with our legs around everybody, one in back of

41

bot-tom of my soul and I tried, _____ I tried.

Spoken: *Everyone is going:* *"Woosh... I feel the snow, I feel the cold...the air."* *And Mr. Karp*

turns to me and says: "O.K. Morales, what did you feel?" *Sung:* And I said, "Noth-ing, __

Vamp under dialogue

I'm feel-ing noth-ing," __ and he says, "Noth-ing __ could

get a girl trans-ferred!" They all felt some-thing, —

but I felt noth-ing — ex - cept the

feel - ing that this bull - shit was ab - surd! *Spoken: But I said to myself:*

"Hey!, it's only the first week. Maybe it's genetic. They don't have bob sleds in San Juan."

"Noth-ing!"_ And Karp al - lowed it, which real - ly makes me

burn. They were so help - ful. They called me

hope - less. Un - til I real - ly did - n't know where else to

turn! *Spoken: And Karp kept saying: "Morales, I think you should transfer to girls' high.*

help me feel it. Pret-ty please!"_____ And a

voice from down at the bot-tom of my soul came up _____ to the top of my head. _ And the

voice from down at the bot-tom of my soul, here is what_____ it

said: "This man is noth-ing! _ This course is

SHOW OFF
from *The Drowsy Chaperone*

Words and Music by Lisa Lambert
and Greg Morrison

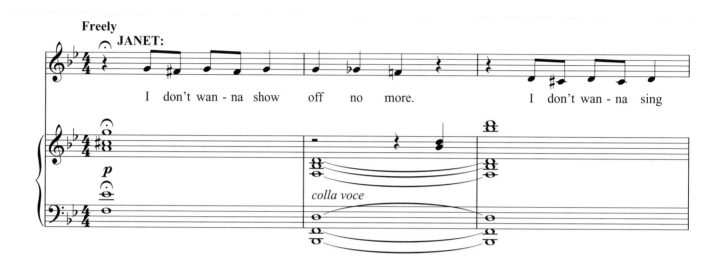

I don't wan-na show off no more. I don't wan-na sing

tunes no more. I don't wan-na ride moons no more.

I don't wan-na show off I don't wan-na wear

Janet is joined by chorus in this number, edited here as a solo.

this no more ___ play the sauc - y Swiss miss no more ___

blow my sig - na-ture *(kiss)* no more. I don't wan - na show

off. Don't try to con - trol me

I've made up my mind And that's

SHY
from *Once Upon a Mattress*

Words by Marshall Barer
Music by Mary Rodgers

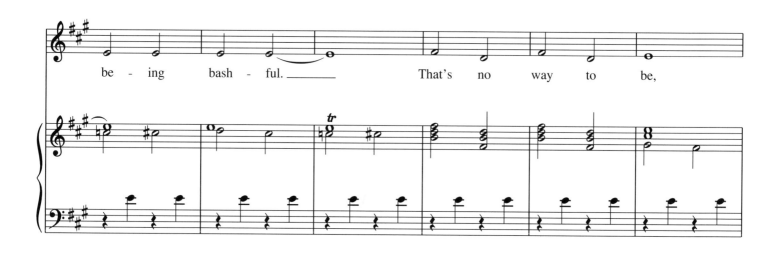

And you may be sure: _____ way down deep I'm de-mure. _____ Though some peo-ple I know might de-ny it, At bot-tom I'm qui-et and pure! _____ I'm a-ware that it's wrong _____ to be meek as I am; My chanc-es may pass me by. I pre-tend to be

strong _____ but as weak as I am, All I can do is try. God knows I

try! _____ Though I'm fright-ened and shy _____

___ And de-spite the im - pres-sion I give, I con - fess that I'm liv - ing a

lie, _____ Be - cause I'm ac-tual-ly ter - ri - bly ti - mid and hor - ri - bly

Rubato

Moderate 2

shy. _____ Though a

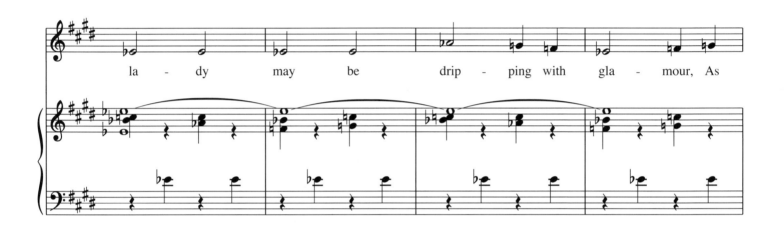

la - dy may be drip - ping with gla - mour, As

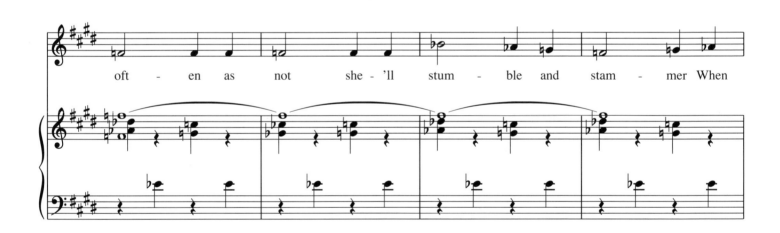

oft - en as not she'll stum - ble and stam - mer When

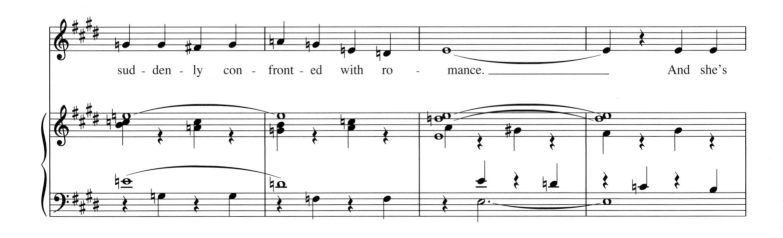

sud - den - ly con - front - ed with ro - mance. _____ And she's

like-ly to fall on her face _____ When she's

fi - nal-ly face to face with a pair of pants.

Quite oft-en the la - dy's not as

hard to please as she seems. _____ Quite

oft - en she'll set - tle for some - thing less than the man of her

dreams.

I'm go - ing fish - ing for a mate.

I'm gon - na look in ev - 'ry nook.

But how much long - er must I wait   With bait - ed breath and ho - ok?   And that is why, _____ Though I'm pain - ful - ly shy, _____ I'm in - sane to know

Più mosso - Charleston beat

Which sir?__   You, sir __ Not you, sir. __ Then who, sir?__

Where, sir ___ And when, sir? ___ I could - n't ___ be ten - ser, ___ So

Let's get ___ this done, man. ___ Get on with ___ the fun, man.

I am one man shy. ___

Jazz 4

A TRIP TO THE LIBRARY

from *She Loves Me*

Words by Sheldon Harnick
Music by Jerry Bock

MISS RITTER: *(Spoken before the introduction) Let me tell you, you've never seen anything like that library. So many books. . . so much marble. . . so quiet!*

start-ed to reach for a book and my hand aut-o-mat-i-c'lly came to a stop.

I

don't know how long I stood fro-zen, a vic-tim of pan-ic and mor-ti-fi-ca-tion.

With Freedom

Oh, _____ how I want-ed to flee _____ when a kind-ly voice, a

rall.

Moderato

gen-tle voice whis-pered "Par-don me."

And there _ was this dear, sweet, clear-ly re - spec - ta - ble thick-ly be - spec - ta-cled

man who stood _ by my side and qui - et - ly said _ to me "Ma'am,

Don't mean _ to in - trude, but I was just won - der-ing are you in need _ of some

help?" I said "no . . . Yes, I am!"

mf (*mf*)

The next __ thing I know I'm sip-ping hot choc - 'late and

tell-ing my trou - bles to Paul, whose ten - der brown eyes kept send-ing com-pas - sion-ate

looks. A trip __ to the li - brar - y _____ has made _ a new

girl of __ me, _____ for sud - den-ly I can __ see ____ the mag - ic of

books.   I

have to ad-mit in the back of my mind, I was pray-ing he would-n't get fresh.   And

all of the while I was won-der-ing why an il - lit - er-ate girl should at - tract him.   Then

all of a sud-den he said that I could-n't go wrong with "The Way of All Flesh."   Of

course, it's a nov-el, but I did-n't know or I cer-tain-ly would-n't have smacked him. _____ Well, he gave me a

smile, _____ that I could-n't re - sist, _____ and I knew at once how

much I liked this op - tom - e - trist.

rall. **Moderato**

mf

You know_ what this dear, sweet, slight-ly be-spec - ta-cled gen-tle-man said _ to me

next? He said __ he could solve this prob-lem of mine. __ I said "How?"

He said __ if I'd like he'd will-ing-ly read __ to me some of his fa - vor-ite

things. I said "When?" He said "Now." His nov - el ap -

proach seemed high-ly sus-pi - cious and pos-si-bly dan - ger-ous too. I told __ my-self

wait, think, dare you go up ___ to his flat. What hap - pens if

things go ___ wrong? ___ It's ob - vi - ous he's quite ___ strong. ___ He read ___ to me

all night ___ long, ___ now how ___ a-bout that!

rall.

Rubato **Deliberately**

It's hard ___ to be - lieve how

rall.

tru - ly do - mes - tic and hap - pi - ly hope - ful I feel. I pic - ture my Paul there

read-ing a - loud _ as I cook. As long _ as he's there to _ read _ there's quite _ a good

chance in - deed, _ a chance _ that I'll nev - er _ need _ to o - pen a

book! Un-like _ some-one else some-one I dim-ly re - call.

I know he'll on - ly have eyes for _ me, _ my op - tom - e - trist Paul. _____

STEPSISTERS' LAMENT
from *Cinderella*

Lyrics by Oscar Hammerstein II
Music by Richard Rodgers

Why would a fel-low want a girl like her, a frail and fluf-fy beau - ty?

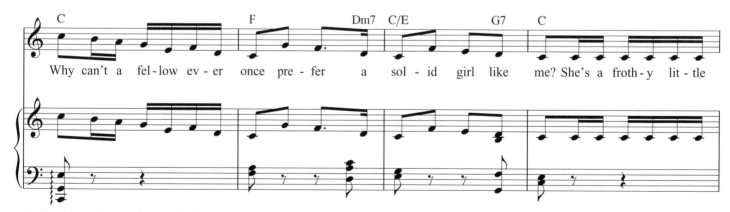

Why can't a fel-low ev - er once pre-fer a sol - id girl like me? She's a froth-y lit - tle

In the show this song is sung by both sisters.

TAYLOR, THE LATTE BOY

Lyrics by Marcy Heisler
Music by Zina Goldrich

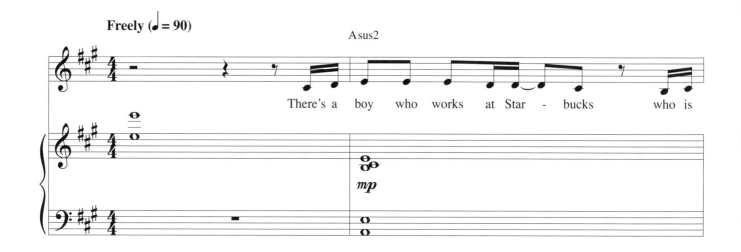

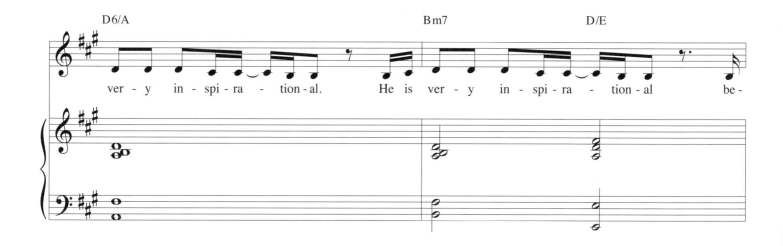

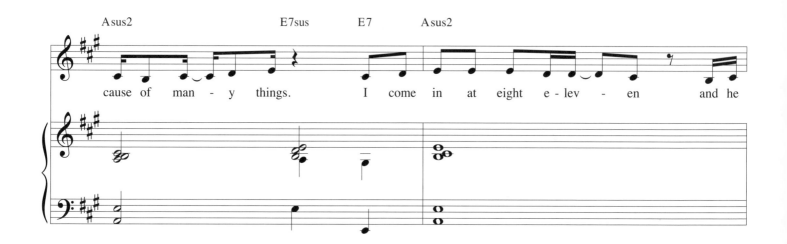

*pronounced "pome"

WHATEVER HAPPENED TO MY PART?

from *Monty Python's Spamalot*

Lyrics by Eric Idle
Music by John Du Prez and Eric Idle

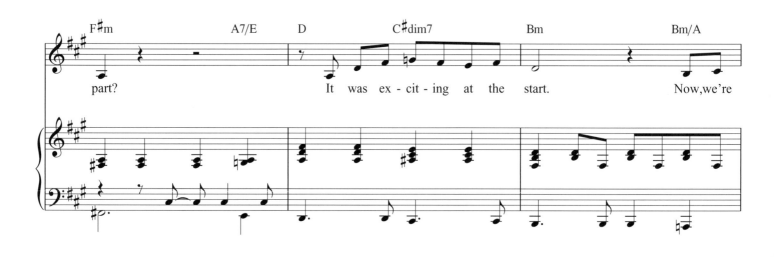